Pages Of Renewal

Inspiration for Life's Journey

Jacob Munson

BookLeaf
Publishing

India | USA | UK

Made with ❤ on the BookLeaf Publishing Platform
www.bookleafpub.in
www.bookleafpub.com

Dedication

To Ashley who had encouraged
me to take this leap of faith.

Preface

In the pages that follow, you will find poems born of both sunlight and shadows. These verses trace the arc of childhood innocence confronted by heartbreak, faith discovered in the quiet corners of despair, and hearts refined by the warmth of God's everlasting promises. Whether recalling a childhood kingdom built of branches and earth or wrestling with doubts that weigh heavy on the soul, each poem offers a glimpse of our universal quest for meaning and grace. May these reflections invite you to remember the wonder of your own beginnings, acknowledge the storms you've weathered, and lean into a love that makes all things new.

Acknowledgements

To anyone who picks up this book in search of comfort, truth, or understanding—thank you for reading. May you find at least a thread of encouragement in these pages.

Whispering Pines

We built forts in the whispering pines,
Walls of branches, floors of earth.
Back then, the outdoors was our kingdom,
The forest floor our throne.

Morning light crowned us sovereigns,
No boundaries, the days stretched endless.
Our laughter echoing like birdsong,
Glories awaited beyond the bend.

We swore by the meadow's hush,
We'd keep our kingdoms intact.
But soon days began to fold in,
Like pages in an ancient story,

Where the hero grows older,
Wonder dimming at the edges.
Still, for one bright afternoon,
The sun warmed our wonder.

The Flicker of Innocence

Each sunrise was a new invitation,
To laugh and run, or hide and seek.
We chased each other through fields of gold,
Scattering leaves with careless ease.

Afternoons bloomed like daisies in the yard,
Even chores held a certain air of joy.
But even daisies wither in the fold of dusk,
And daydreams slip through parted fingers.

Yet the flicker of that first light remains,
It never truly dies.
Like a boat on a quiet river,
It yearns to set sail at dawn.

Yes, the shadows may gather,
But the song of possibility,
Like a gentle current urging us forward,
Waits to be sung once more.

The Library of Life

In the library of life, we roam stacks of stories,
Words come alive at the turn of every page.
Some tales are bold, others half-lived.
A mosaic of sorrow and delight around every corner.

Puzzles appear in every twist, each turn invites
transformation.
Chaos births yearning, a call for deeper meaning.
Each question shapes the need for understanding,
As we seek the Author's hand among the lines.

From childhood's bright skies to nights of grief,
Each chapter etches its lessons on our spirit.
Ink inscribes our choices on time's tender pages,
Trusting each question leads us towards truth.

So let us keep reading, and decipher life's riddles,
For in these chapters, we glimpse an eternal Word.
A promise that holds our future in His hands,
The mystery of being, the promise of love.

Pieces of Ourselves

We give up little pieces of ourselves,
Grasping at images of empty dreams.
But pieces are not peace.
That calm we crave is bigger, deeper.

A vast pit stretched endless.
We clutch our ambitions,
Thinking we can shape reality to fit,
Our narrow, selfish intentions.

Yet the harder we cling,
The more the cracks in our façade show.
If you truly want His peace,
Place everything at His feet.

Only then will you find,
A fresh page awaits each dawn.
For your name is written firmly,
In the Book of Life.

Cracks in the Concrete

Neon lights flicker, promising gold,
Yet cost more than they're worth.
We work the corner of shadows,
Selling illusions, buying regret.

Doing anything to pay rent,
But doubt and deceit tug at our sleeves.
Dreams slam the sidewalk with a hollow thud,
Falling through cracks in the concrete.

No brand can patch what's broken inside,
Only faith can mend the hidden seams.
Past broken rubble and weary steps,
The promise of hope endures.

A quiet flame murmurs in the hush of despair,
Whispering that all is not lost.
From this wreckage, a seed of renewal,
Proof your darkest hours can lead to rebirth.

Quiet Battles

Sometimes heartbreak feels like a battle,
But the battleground is inside.
Weapons are words unspoken,
Regrets that slash the night.

We imagine a perfect pair,
Like a fairy tale.
But real stories twist and turn,
And leave you wondering where.

Where did it all go wrong,
Where did the end begin.
Rain falls heavy in the hush of 2 a.m.,
Washing illusions away.

Yet in that flood, new soil forms,
Where seeds of hope can grow.
Hold on to that tender shoot;
Let sorrow pave a brighter road.

Unreceived Love

I made moves for you,
But you chose another road.
My heart poured itself out
On parched earth, unreceived.

You couldn't wait for me,
You fled as if set free.
Midnight hours I plead your name,
Silence was the echo left behind.

Reality's teeth bite deep.
The ache at remained still.
Yet somehow, I sensed a quiet comfort,
A voice that never left me.

God's mercy is deeper than heartbreak,
Steadier than any grounds that quake.
In the end, I found resilience,
To watch the sunrise one more time.

8. Rust

I imagined perfection, a future so bright,
But your view of me never saw that light.
My heart turned to dust, your love to rust,
Dreams hollowed out by neglect.

Tears were my only assurance,
A thunderstorm in my soul.
Yet in my pain, I heard a voice,
Breaking through the gloom.

A whisper of hope, faint but clear:
"You're not alone; you were made for more."
Sometimes devastation is a forging fire,
That reveals gold beneath the tarnish.

Life moves in cycles: decay, then bloom.
New love awaits to see me whole.
So, I'll say farewell to what was never there,
And embrace God's light unburdened.

Through Oliver's Eyes

I see Oliver Twist in every hungry face,
Begging, "Please, sir, I want some more."
Reaching for a piece of that pie,
That's served up in crooked rations.

The more we strive, the emptier we feel,
A hollow ache deep in our bones.
They talk of opportunity,
But greed locks the door.

Kicking you out to stand in the cold,
Waiting for kindness from shuttered windows.
Look close and you'll see the system:
A heartless clock, ticking profits.

Yet hope flickers, faint but fierce,
Like a candle in a grim alley.
In a soft prayer, in an outstretched hand,
We find abundance in God's grace.

Heavy Debt

All of the lights in the sky, they promise,
Will lead you to fame and riches unending.
But they are only illusions of the shadows,
On the cave wall we perceive as reality.

We try to outrun our heavy debt,
Only to find it around each corner.
But let go of your heavy burdens,
And run to the one who welcomes the weary.

For He will make your burden light,
And lead you past corruption's glare.
Kneel not before greed's table;
A better feast lies in the unseen.

Somewhere beyond this false façade,
A golden compass points true north,
Hold onto faith when you're at your darkest,
Knowing light will always win in the end.

Dry Rivers

Rivers once roared behind my eyes,
My tears flowed without shame.
Yet time taught them to run dry,
Taught me to hold them in.

Soon the desert took hold,
Brittle dust replacing tears.
Still, in the quiet cracks,
I felt God stir a hidden spring,

Reminding me that drought isn't forever.
A single shower can awaken the soil,
Make flowers blossom in arid fields.
So I let tears come again,

Freed by the promise of gentle renewal,
For even deserts can bloom after the rain.
My heart, once cracked, drinks in grace,
Embracing each raindrop as it falls.

Breaking the Cycle

I saw my father lost to the bottle,
My mother praying for deliverance.
I swore I'd break the cycle,
But it chased me down the block,

Tried to wrap me in the same old chains.
Night after night, I wrestled,
With ghosts in every glass,
Drinking shame with every drop.

But I turned each dawn into a vow,
And laid my brokenness at God's feet.
The chains that tried to hold me back,
Soon began to crack.

I saw the path to freedom open wide,
And with trembling, I walked it.
With each small step forward,
Hope glowed brighter than the sun.

A Gentle Knock

A gentle knock inside my heart,
I once tried to ignore.
Night after night, the knock persisted,
Would not leave me alone.

Finally, one night I listened,
And opened up the door.
I found there waiting for me,
My Savior and my Lord.

In that moment my burdens lifted,
Replaced by wings of faith.
For only those who seek and listen,
Will find God's loving grace.

Why push away the One whose spirit,
Calls you to be His own?
He knocks and waits for all who listen,
To guide us to our home.

Surrendering Ambitions

We give up only a little piece,
Still craving a peace the size,
Of our own selfish ambition,
Our eyes set on some prize.

Trying to mold God to our purpose.
Will never satisfy.
Taking only what suits us.
Only feeds the lie.

The weight of our illusions,
Crushes us ever the more.
Hand Him over everything.
And find rest for your soul,

Don't ever say you're too far gone;
You're never out of reach.
Stop playing the same old song,
Sing a new melody.

Second Chances

They say life offers no reruns,
But mercy tells another story.
Grace arrives with each sunrise,
A blank slate after midnight's regrets.

Countless times, I stumbled,
Certain the door was closed for good.
Then morning's light proved me wrong,
Tender, forgiving, unwavering.

Every failure can become a seed,
If planted in the soil of faith.
We grow upward, day by day,
Carrying scars that blossom into wisdom.

And so we live a thousand rebirths,
Never out of reach of God's embrace.
At dawn, hope kneels at sorrow's door,
Then rises in mercy, renewed once more.

Chameleon

I wore so many masks,
Trying to fit in,
That I didn't know the real me,
Just a chameleon.

The mirror shows us our own reflections,
But I didn't see mine.
All I saw were even more questions,
I was running out of time.

But then God opened up my eyes,
Made it very clear,
That what I saw were simply lies,
There was nothing I should fear.

I finally saw how God sees me,
I am perfect in His sight.
Now I stand unashamed and free,
Walking boldly in His light.

Ash

Love once burned bright,
Then flickered, to ash.
I held that ash,
In cupped palms,

Afraid to let it scatter.
But it grew heavier,
The more I held on,
Dragging me with its weight.

I breathed a sigh,
And let it go,
Not knowing,
If more awaits.

But in letting it go,
I made room,
For an ember to spark,
Something new.

Living Water

In a land of thirst,
I wandered, parched,
Looking for an oasis.
At the bottom of a bottle,

Or the edge of a pill.
But my soul found dryness,
At every,
Twist and turn.

Then came a voice,
Calling from the desert:
"Come to Me,
All who thirst."

At once I ran towards that voice,
I sipped from the well.
And living water,
Quenched me from within.

A Quiet Prayer

Prayers can feel silent,
When you feel it's the end,
When resolve dwindles,
And the darkness closes in.

But they summon Heaven's armies,
Angels step in from the margins.
They carry your spirit,
Lift you out of despair.

Remember always,
You are never alone.
When scripture is spoken,
When you call out His name.

For even in the darkest corridor,
He who formed the stars guides us on.
Victory isn't always thunder,
Sometimes it's a quiet prayer.

Mercies New

In each worn face on the street,
A flicker of childlike wonder remains,
Though battered by time's cruelty.
We hold onto eternity.

Yes, the world tries to break you down,
But each morning He renews the vow:
"My mercies are new every sunrise."
From that promise, we draw breath,

Stand a little straighter,
Look a little farther.
Dark corners can't hide forever;
Light breaks in.

When words fail, remember,
The cross gave us a home.
Let worry slide off your shoulders,
And breathe freely again.

Final Words

I stand at the edge of this story,
Pages fluttering in the wind.
Scars may mark your story,
But each one speaks of grace.

If I've learned anything,
It's that brokenness
Can birth beauty,
That God's love redeems.

Every passing hour,
Every shattered dream,
We don't walk alone,
Through each valley.

His promises hold true.
And so I close this chapter,
With grateful tears,
Ready for what comes next.